D0732686

How to Hear God
Bill Hybels

InterVarsity Press
P.O. Box 1400, Downers Grove, IL 60515-1426
World Wide Web: www.ivpress.com
E-mail: email@ivpress.com

*InterVarsity Press® is the book-publishing division of InterVarsity Christian
Fellowship/USA®, a student movement active on campus at hundreds of
universities, colleges and schools of nursing in the United States of America,
and a member movement of the International Fellowship of Evangelical
Students. For information about local and regional activities, write Public
Relations Dept., InterVarsity Christian Fellowship/USA, 6400 Schroeder
Rd., P.O. Box 7895, Madison, WI 53707-7895, or visit the IVCF website at
<www.intervarsity.org>.*

The material in this booklet is taken from Too Busy Not to Pray *by Bill
Hybels (InterVarsity Press).*

All Scripture quotations, unless otherwise indicated, are taken from the Holy
Bible, New International Version®. NIV®. *Copyright ©1973, 1978,
1984 by International Bible Society. Used by permission of Zondervan
Publishing House. All rights reserved.*

ISBN-10: 0-87784-059-8
ISBN-13: 978-0-87784-059-6

Printed in the United States of America ∞

P	19	18	17	16	15	14	13	12	11
Y	15	14	13	12	11	10	09	08	

I was once attending a conference in Southern California where, for some strange reason in the middle of one afternoon, I felt a leading from God that I ought to attend a certain workshop — one in which I had very little interest. The workshop was in a different building, and as I was walking to it, I met a young man and started talking with him.

As we talked, I was impressed by his tender spirit, and I realized God was knitting our hearts together. Over the course of several months, we corresponded and then visited one another. Eventually he joined our church staff, and many people think he is the most effective minister to high-school students in the country.

When God tells us to write to this person or make an appointment with that person or give away so much money, to start this or stop that or share the other thing, it doesn't have to make sense to us. Some of the most important decisions in my life have made no sense at all from a worldly perspective. But I have learned that I can't afford not to respond to his leadings. So if God tells you to do something, do it! Trust him! Take the risk!

A lot of Christians don't expect God to speak to them. By their actions you would expect that Jesus packed up and went back to heaven forty days after his resurrection and hasn't been heard from since. Though this attitude is common, it does not fit the picture of God painted throughout Scripture. The Holy Spirit is ready, willing and able to communicate with us. According to Scripture, he leads, rebukes, affirms, comforts and assures Christ's followers.

Private Promptings
A few years ago, after a particularly exhausting

meeting, I got into my car and drove out of the church parking lot onto the exit road. As I started down the road, out of the corner of my eye I saw someone walking toward the parking area. In that fraction of a second I received what I thought was a leading from God—to go offer some form of assistance to the person I had just passed.

My initial response was *Why?* The person didn't seem to be having any difficulty. My second response was *Why me?* I'd already done my share that day, studying, working on a sermon, counseling with people and then leading a meeting. I wanted to go home.

And so I kept driving, rationalizing my disobedience to the little leading from God. But the Holy Spirit persisted. By the time I had reached the entrance sign, I felt so restless in my spirit that I said, "I can't put up with this anymore. Disobedience is causing more stress than simply turning around and obeying, even if I'm tired and don't know why I'm supposed to do this."

So I headed back down the entrance road,

pulled up alongside the person, who was still walking south, rolled my window down and awkwardly said, "Is there any way I can serve you? Could I drive you to your car?" (Our parking lot is large, and frequently people forget where they have parked.)

The woman, whom I had never seen before, gladly accepted my offer. Just as she was about to thank me and get out of the car, she said, "There was an announcement in the bulletin tonight about the need for administrative help in the church office, and I've been feeling God leading me to apply for that position. What do you think?"

We discussed the matter briefly, and then we each drove off. That night I had no idea how offering help to a person who probably didn't need it would affect my life and ministry. As it turned out, the woman joined our staff and served faithfully for almost ten years. I wonder what would have happened if I hadn't obeyed that leading.

It makes no sense to believe that God lost his

voice at the end of the first century. If the essence of Christianity is a personal relationship between the almighty God and individual human beings, it stands to reason that God still speaks to believers today. You can't build a relationship on one-way speeches. You need frequent, sustained, intimate contact between two persons, both of whom speak and both of whom listen.

I could tell story after story of leadings God has entrusted to me and to others. I could describe the dramatic effects of obeying God's leadings—or of ignoring them. But such stories may not be to the point. The real question is this: what are you going to do about the leadings *you* receive?

Once a person turns his or her life over to Jesus Christ, it is no longer business as usual. Life no longer consists only of that which can be seen or smelled or felt or figured out by human logic. It includes walking by faith, and that means opening oneself to the miraculous ministry of the Holy Spirit.

Paul wrote, "You . . . are controlled . . . by the Spirit, if the Spirit of God lives in you. And if anyone does not have the Spirit of Christ, he does not belong to Christ" (Romans 8:9). He told believers to "live by the Spirit," to be "led by the Spirit," to "keep in step with the Spirit" (Galatians 5).

It's an honor to be able to speak to God. We don't have to go through a priest or a saint or any other intermediary. We don't have to follow any prescribed rituals. We don't have to wait for an appointment. Anywhere, anytime, under any circumstances, we can "approach the throne of grace with confidence, so that we may receive mercy and find grace to help us in our time of need" (Hebrews 4:16).

It's ironic, though, that most of the time we think of prayer as talking to God, rarely stopping to wonder whether God might want to talk to us. But as I've studied prayer and prayed, I've sensed God saying, "If we enjoy a relationship, why are you the one doing all the talking? Let *me* get a word in somewhere!"

The Importance of Listening

Listening to God speak to us through his Holy Spirit is not only normal, but it is essential.

People who are really interested in hearing from God must pay a price: they must discipline themselves to be still before God. This is not an easy task, but it is essential. Psalm 46:10 says, "Be still, and know that I am God."

Jesus developed the discipline of stillness before God in spite of his extremely busy life. Crowds followed him wherever he went. Daily he preached and taught and healed. It was hard for him to find time alone to pray, and he had to get up long before dawn to do it. "Very early in the morning, while it was still dark, Jesus got up, left the house and went off to a solitary place, where he prayed" (Mark 1:35).

Times of stillness and solitude were important to Jesus. In those times of seclusion he not only poured out his heart to the Father, he earnestly listened to him as well. He needed his Father's comfort, direction, affirmation and assurance. Because of the continual leadings he received from the Father, there was purpose to his steps. The people around him saw his confidence and certainty, and they were amazed "because he taught them as one who had authority" (Mark 1:22).

Strength from Solitude

God's power is available to us when we come to him in solitude, when we learn how to focus and center our hearts and be quiet before him. When we learn the discipline of stillness before God, we find that his leadings come through to us clearly, with little interference.

That is why I have made the commitment to spend from half an hour to an hour every single morning in a secluded place with the Lord. It is one of the handful of spiritual disciplines I have ever really stuck with, and I am not tempted to abandon it, because it has made my life so much richer.

After I reflect on the previous day and write out my prayers, my spirit is quiet and receptive. That is when I write an *L* for *listen* on a piece of paper and circle it. Then I sit quietly and simply say, "Now, Lord, I invite you to speak to me by your Holy Spirit."

The moments with God that follow are the ones that really matter.

Power comes out of stillness; strength comes out of solitude. Decisions that change the entire course of your life come out of the holy of holies, your times of stillness before God.

I like my way of quieting my mind and preparing myself to hear God speak; it works well for me. But I know it won't work for everyone. Some people can't stand writing anything, let alone journals and prayers. They may prefer to talk quietly to God and then have a period of listening.

The important thing is not to follow a particular method but to find a way that works for you. Custom-design an approach that will still your racing mind and body, soften your heart and enable you to hear God's still, small voice. Then, when you are centered and focused on God, invite him to speak to you.

Questions for God

I have several questions I regularly ask God. Depending on your situation, you might ask:

"What's the next step in developing my character?"

"What educational goals should I aim at?"

"What's the next step in my family?"

"What's the next step in my ministry?"

"What's the next step in my vocation?"

"In what direction should my dating relationship go?"

"What should I do for my children?"

"How should I plan my giving?"

Whatever you ask the Lord, you will be amazed at the way he leads. In the solitude and stillness, what might God say to you?

To some seekers God might say, "You've been reading Christian books and going to Christian meetings long enough. Now it's time you became a Christian. Come to me, repent of your sin and enter into a faith-oriented relationship with me."

To those who have already made that commitment he might say, "Return to me. You've been stumbling around. Let's get reacquainted!"

To people facing trials he might offer words of comfort: "I'm right here. I know your name, and I know your pain. I'm going to give you strength, so trust me."

And to still others, this message might come: "Follow my leading and take a risk. Walk with me toward new horizons."

The message will be suited to the person's individual need, but the central truth is certain: We serve a God who has spoken in history, who still speaks today and who wants to speak to us.

When God Is Silent

But what if no message comes through?

Sometimes, when I wait quietly for God to speak, I sense total silence from heaven. It's as if no one's home. Did I ask the wrong question? Was I foolish to expect answers? Was God really listening?

I've concluded that I don't need to feel upset if sometimes God chooses to remain silent. He's a living Being, not an answering machine, and he speaks when he has something to say.

Sometimes I ask my wife, "Is there anything you want to tell me that we haven't had time to sit down and talk about?" My question gives Lynne the opportunity to tell me anything she wants, but it doesn't force her to talk. Sometimes she says, "No, nothing in particular." And that's fine.

More often than not, though, she does have a message for me—and so does God, when I invite him to speak.

I know that God continues to speak to his people today, and I am convinced that there are two reasons we don't hear his voice more often. The most obvious reason is that *we don't listen for it*. We don't schedule times of stillness that make communication possible.

Be honest with yourself. When do you turn off the TV, the radio, the CD player and listen to nothing louder than the refrigerator's hum? When do you make yourself quiet and available to God? When do you formally invite him to speak to you?

Do you build the discipline of solitude right into your schedule? Try it! Like any new practice, it will feel awkward at first. Gradually it will become more natural, and eventually you will feel off balance if you don't make time for solitude every day.

Tuned In to God's Voice

In addition to carving out blocks of time to listen to God, do you keep your ears tuned to him each day?

It is possible to develop a sensitivity to the Holy Spirit's still, small voice. It is possible to be aware throughout the day, even while going about your daily work, of God's gentle promptings. That's what it means to "live by the Spirit" (Galatians 5:16).

These on-the-spot promptings are not a substitute for unhurried quiet time with God. In fact, they tend to come to me only when I regularly make time for stillness and solitude. But when they come, they're wonderful.

The other reason we may not hear God's voice is that *we don't plan to do anything about it.* God speaks; we listen, nod and say, "How interesting!" But if we don't follow up on the Holy Spirit's leadings, he may see no reason to continue speaking.

One morning an elder of my church called me on the phone and said, "I had a leading to call you. Are you in trouble or anything?"

"Not that I know of," I said.

"All right," she said. "I'm just obeying the Lord. I wanted to call you and encourage you."

I was glad she called, even if neither of us knew exactly why. I never object to being encouraged, and I was glad she was obedient to the Holy Spirit. When God tells us to do something, as long as it's within the limits set by Scripture, we don't have to understand it. All we need to do is obey and trust God to use our obedience to accomplish his will.

Is It Really from God?
Sometimes people will say to me, "I believe in

leadings. But how can I be sure that a leading is truly from God?"

This is a valid question. The Bible warns us that Satan, the evil one, is capable of both issuing his own leadings for destructive purposes and undermining God's leadings in your life.

Paul wrote to Timothy, "The Spirit clearly says that in later times some will abandon the faith and follow deceiving spirits and things taught by demons" (1 Timothy 4:1).

These lying spirits may appear to be channels of God's power. Jesus predicted that "false Christs and false prophets" would "perform great signs and miracles to deceive even the elect—if that were possible" (Matthew 24:24).

Evil spirits are not necessarily easy to distinguish from God's ministering spirits, the angels. As Paul pointed out, "Satan himself masquerades as an angel of light" (2 Corinthians 11:14). It is very important to know the origin of the leadings coming into your mind.

Adam and Eve followed a leading to increase their knowledge by eating an attractive fruit, and they plunged the human race into darkness and misery (Genesis 3). King David followed a leading to befriend a beautiful army wife, and it cost him his best general and a son (2 Samuel 11—12).

Who led Timothy McVeigh to bomb the Oklahoma Federal Building, or thirty-nine Heaven's Gate cult members to commit suicide? Who leads one group to execute another in the name of ethnic cleansing, or the Ku Klux Klan to throw rocks and bottles at their neighbors because their neighbors' skin is darker than their own?

Who leads me to say hurtful things, to be arrogant, to color the truth? Who prompts me to care less about serving others than about my own advancement and fulfillment?

Heavenly Warfare

In Ephesians 6:10-18 Paul reminds us that there's a war going on in this universe. "Put on the full armor of God," he says, "so that you can take your stand against the devil's schemes.

For our struggle is not against flesh and blood, but against . . . the spiritual forces of evil in the heavenly realms" (vv. 11-12).

This war is being waged on the spiritual battlefields of our minds. As God leads people for his glory and for their benefit, Satan does everything in his power to undo God's work and undermine his activity in people's lives. Because of this spiritual war, it is possible that some of the notions that come into our heads have been authored in hell, not heaven.

So how can you be sure where a particular leading is coming from?

In 1 John 4:1 we read, "Dear friends, do not believe every spirit, but test the spirits to see whether they are from God, because many false prophets have gone out into the world." I'm going to suggest three criteria by which to test leadings you receive.

Consistent with Scripture
First, *all leadings that come from God are consistent with God's Word, the Bible.*

The surest way to test the source of a leading is to check it against Scripture. As I interact with people in my church, almost every month someone tells me he is being led to be unfaithful to his wife. This is not a leading from God! I can say that unequivocally. Listen to what God says:

> [The LORD] no longer pays attention to your offerings or accepts them with pleasure from your hands. You ask, "Why?" It is because the LORD is acting as the witness between you and the wife of your youth, because you have broken faith with her, though she is your partner, the wife of your marriage covenant. . . . "I hate divorce," says the LORD God of Israel. (Malachi 2:13-14, 16)

A leading to be unfaithful to your spouse is never a leading from God. Neither is a leading to cheat on an examination, to exaggerate to a customer, to spread hurtful gossip, to deceive your parents or children or to do anything else forbidden by Scripture.

If the leading goes against the Bible, it obviously comes from an unholy spirit. Dismiss it summarily. There is no other Christian way to deal with an unscriptural leading.

Consistent with God's Gifts

If a leading is not contrary to Scripture, it's time to look at the second criterion: *God's leadings are usually consistent with the person he made you to be.*

Some people seem to think that God creates a person with certain gifts and then expects the person to excel in totally unrelated fields. I've met people who adore math and computers and do very well in those areas, but they assume God is leading them into music or theology.

Some people who love the outdoors and don't really come alive unless they're in nature nevertheless assume God is leading them toward a downtown office job on the thirty-fifth floor of a high-rise.

I've even met people who are uncomfortable around children and still think God is leading them to become schoolteachers.

I ask these people, "Why do you assume

God's leadings would contradict who he made you to be? Why would he design you for one purpose and then ask you to fulfill another?"

Our God is purposeful. He is the master orchestrator and synthesizer of the universe. To be sure, he loves to stretch our abilities and expand our potential, and that often involves leading us along untried paths. That does not mean, however, that he ignores our gifts and inherent interests. After all, he gave them to us in the first place so that we could serve him more effectively! Instead, he strengthens our natural abilities and builds on them.

You matter to God. He made you, and he knows what will fulfill you. He knows what vocation is best suited to your talents and abilities. He knows if you should marry or remain single, and if you marry, he knows which marriage partner is best suited to you. He knows what church you can flourish in. And this is what he says to you: "I want to guide your life. I know the path that will glorify me and be productive for you, and I want to put you on it."

If you sense a leading that seems completely contrary to who God made you to be, I advise you to test it very carefully. Is God asking you to do this difficult thing because there is simply no one else who will do it? Is he asking you to stretch into new areas so that your unique gifts will grow? Or is this perhaps not a God-inspired leading at all but rather a distraction from the task God has given you to do?

The Servanthood Dimension

Third, *God's leadings usually involve servanthood.* I find that many counterfeit leadings are fairly easy to discern because they are self-promoting or self-serving. It never fails—in late January or early February when the Midwest goes into the deep freeze, I feel a strange but compelling calling to start a church in Honolulu.

Over the years I've found that if a leading promises easy money and fame and perks and toys, I'd better watch out. Prosperity has ruined more people than servanthood and adversity ever will. On the other hand, I can usually sense that a leading is from the Holy Spirit when it calls me to humble myself, serve somebody, encourage somebody or give something away. Very rarely will the evil one lead us to do those kinds of things.

This is what Paul told the Ephesian elders about one of his leadings: "Now, compelled by the Spirit, I am going to Jerusalem, not knowing what will happen to me there. I only know that in every city the Holy Spirit warns me that prison and hardships are facing me" (Acts 20:22-23). Paul was not being asked to do something contrary to his gifts—all the way to Jerusalem he would be preaching the gospel and strengthening young churches. He was, however, being asked to sacrifice safety and comfort for the sake of the kingdom.

Not every leading from God will involve pain and sacrifice, but expect that quite often God's leadings will mean making gut-wrenching decisions that test the limits of your faith and make you face life's ultimate issues head-on. Many of God's leadings will require you to choose between being comfortable and building a godly character, between amassing money and seeking first God's kingdom, between being a winner in the world's eyes and being a winner in God's eyes.

So if a leading promises you overnight health, wealth, comfort and happiness, be cautious. God led Jesus to a cross, not a crown, and yet that cross ultimately proved to be the gateway to freedom and forgiveness for every sinner in the world. God also asks us as Jesus' followers to carry a cross. Paradoxically, in carrying that cross we find liberty and joy and fulfillment.

Proceed with Caution

Thus you can conclude that a leading is probably from God if it is consistent with his Word, if it is consistent with who he made you to be and if it requires some sacrifice or steps of faith. Let me add a few cautions:

☐ If a leading requires you to make a major, life-changing decision in a very short period of time, question it.

☐ If a leading requires you to go deeply in debt or place someone else in a position of awkwardness, compromise or danger, question it.

☐ If a leading requires you to compromise family relationships or important friendships, question it.

☐ If a leading creates unrest in the spirit of mature Christian friends or counselors as you share it with them, question it.

Leadings from God can open the door to a fantastically fulfilling Christian adventure, but counterfeit leadings can cause unbelievable amounts of confusion, hardship, pain and trauma.

Test and Obey

It is a terrible loss when Christians are so afraid of counterfeit leadings that they close their ears to the Holy Spirit's leadings too. Not wanting to go off the deep end, they avoid the water altogether. God wants us to test the spirits, of course, but then he wants us to step out in faith and follow him.

Some years ago I had lunch at a restaurant with a man who was not a believer. His friends had told me that he was the toughest, hardest-hitting, most autocratic, hardheaded, hard-hearted man they had ever met. (With a recommendation like that from his friends, I didn't bother to check with his enemies!) Twenty minutes into the meal, I could affirm everything they had said.

We were talking about everything but important things when I felt a leading. The Holy Spirit seemed to whisper to me, "Present the simple truth of Jesus' dying for sinners as clearly as you possibly can—right now."

I didn't want to do that. I thought I knew for certain what his response would be. But the leading was certainly biblical. It fit my gifts, at least under the circumstances, and it was not in any way self-serving! I had a choice: would I trust God, or would I disobey this leading which clearly seemed to be from him?

I obeyed. Abruptly changing the subject, I asked, "Would you like to know how Jesus

Christ takes sinners to heaven?"

"Pardon me?" said the man.

"Point of information," I said. "Would you like to know how Jesus Christ forgives sinners and takes them to heaven?"

"I guess so," he reluctantly agreed.

, So, over dessert, I explained the plan of salvation as plainly and as briefly as I knew how. He asked a few questions. We finished lunch, and I went back to work feeling slightly embarrassed.

Two or three days later I almost fell off my chair when the man called me. He said, "Do you know what I did after our lunch together? I went home, got on my knees and said, 'I'm a sinner in need of a Savior.'"

That man became one of my closest friends. We had seven wonderful years of fellowship together before he went to be with the Lord. And it all can be traced back to a leading.

When you begin to listen for God's leadings, you often won't know why he is asking you to do something. He will lead you down paths through unknown territory, sometimes for no other reason than to teach you to trust him. Remember, the Christian walk is based on faith, not sight (2 Corinthians 5:7), and "without faith it is impossible to please God" (Hebrews 11:6).

For a truly dynamic, authentic, exciting Christian life, listen for the Holy Spirit's leadings. Test them. And then obey them. Roll the spiritual dice. Take a faith gamble. Give it a shot. Cooperate with God. Say yes to him, even if it seems risky or illogical.

People who make opportunities for the Holy Spirit to speak to them know that the Christian life is a continual adventure. If you open your mind and heart to God's leadings, you will be amazed at what he will do. He is more wonderful than you can imagine, and he is attempting to communicate with you more often than you know. You have no idea how much richer and fuller, how much more exciting and more effective your life will be once you make the decision to be still, to be aware and to obey God's leadings.

Further Reading from InterVarsity Press

THE JOY OF LISTENING TO GOD
Joyce Huggett opens up an exciting demension of spiritual life as she explores contemplation, silence and the many ways God speaks to us. *240 pages*

QUIET TIME
This guidebook offers practical methods for developing a regular and meaningful time for fellowship with God. *30 pages*

TOO BUSY NOT TO PRAY
Bill Hybels shows how to slow down to pray, listen to God, respond to what we hear, practice the presence of God and overcome prayer barriers. *191 pages*

MAKING LIFE WORK
Bill Hybels offers practical advice for living the Christian life with wisdom and wholeness. *204 pages*

Bill Hybels *is pastor of Willow Creek Community Church in South Barrington, Illinois.*